Christophe Déceneux

Translation by Wendy Mewes

The Holy Grail and Brocéliande in Dol-Combourg

On the cover, from left to right: Lancelot du Lac in a miniature of the 15th century (BNF-Gallica), the Château de Combourg and, in the hallway of this medieval fortress, the coat of arms of the Coëtquen family. Photographs are by the author, all rights reserved.
For further information, see www.paysdebroceliande.com

Editions BOD 2017

The Château de Combourg and Lake Diane

Each year, the Grail appears illuminated in the cathedral of Dol at midday on the summer solstice, June 21st. Tomb of Thomas James.

The Seigneury of Dol-Combourg

In the middle of the 11th century, a single family ruled over two small neighbouring cities in Brittany: Ginguené (or Junguénée) was the archbishop of Dol-de-Bretagne, at the same time as his young brother Rivallon, first lord of Combourg, was in charge of defending the territory.

Dol and Combourg are situated not far from Mont St-Michel, in a frontier region called the Marches of Brittany, which had the role of defending Armorican territory, frequently challenged in history by the kingdom of France or the Duchy of Normandy.

Today the Château of Combourg is a splendid medieval castle (13th to 15th centuries) attracting many tourists, but at that time it was a simple *motte*, a raised mound of earth topped by a wooden structure. This military presence also protected Dol, with Rivallon in charge of both places as "standard-bearer of Saint Samson". Samson, born in Wales, had been the first bishop of Dol and founder of that parish.

Ginguené also had a major role: Dol was then and had been since the 9th century, the archbishopric of all Brittany, the spiritual centre of the duchy. In the 11th century, the cathedral at Dol was pre-Romanesque, replaced in the 13th century by a most beautiful Gothic edifice, a source of pride today, and rightly so, for the inhabitants of Dol.

Rivallon had three sons, Guillaume, Jean and Gilduin. We can see that the family was very pious: the eldest, Guillaume, was abbot of Saint-Florent de Saumur, the significance of which we shall see later on. Jean was to become, like his uncle, archbishop of Dol and founder of the abbey of Saint-Florent-sous-Dol. Finally, the third brother, called Saint Guildin, refused the bishopric of Dol out of humility and died near Chartres. His relics can be found today at Chartres, as well as at Combourg in the Church of Notre-Dame and the chapel at the château.

From Dol to Monmouth: towards the Arthurian legend

The influence of Saint-Florent de Saumur, where Guillaume, son of Rivallon, was abbot, proved to be very important in the region of Dol. Apart from the Abbaye-sous-Dol already mentioned, we can cite the priory of Saint Florent of Brégain at La Boussac. This village situated between Dol and Mont St-Michel was the fief of a noble family related to the lords of Dol-Combourg. We will elaborate later on the details and references of our research: for now, we just mention the foundation of Brégain by Baderon, and that, more surprising, of Saint-Florent de Monmouth by his brother Guihénoc of Dol. How did Wales come to have a priory dependent on Saint-Florent de Saumur?

Brégain

Rivallon, lord of Combourg, had rather a testy character. He opposed the Duke of Brittany, Conan II, who ordered the siege of Dol. Rivallon appealed for help to Guillaume, Duke of Normandy and future king (William) of England. In 1066 Breton knights accompanied William the Conqueror to Hastings. The new king of England distributed fiefdoms, and that of Monmouth was eventually given to Guihénoc of Dol, who founded the priory of

Saint-Florent of Monmouth there. The little Breton town was thus linked to the Welsh town and remained so for several generations, as the title of seigneury was hereditary. So the origins of both the grandson of Baderon, also called Baderon of Monmouth, and Geoffrey, celebrated creator of the Arthurian legend, each born about 1100 go back to Dol. We know besides that the clerics of Saint Florent pursued their cultural exchanges from both sides of the channel.

The cathedral of Dol (13th century)

Geoffrey of Monmouth invents the Arthurian myth

During the first half of the 12th century, the cleric Geoffrey of Monmouth established the foundations of the myth. He published his *History of the Kings of Britain* (that is to say Great Britain) in about 1135, and then completed the story in 1148 with *The Life of Merlin*, both books being produced in Latin. The author was inspired by Welsh and Armorican (*La Matière de Bretagne*) tales, presenting the context of the Arthurian legend for the first time. Appearing in this *History of the Kings of Britain* are Arthur, queen Guinevere, the magician Merlin, the fairy Morgane, Samson, the seneschal Kay (Keu or Kai), Yvain, Gauvain (Gawain), celebrated knight of the Round Table, and also, the sword Caliburn (later Excaliber), forged on the mystical island of Avalon.

The cathedral of Dol

Here are the characters of the Arthurian cycle, as presented by Geoffrey of Monmouth in the first half of the 12th century:

Geoffrey's Arthurian characters in 1135

Arthur
King of the Britons of England. Geoffrey sets his birth at Tintagel, Cornwall (England), and says he died in 542. From this we can deduce a birth-date in the second half of the 5th century. He is a legendary character, but certain actual war-lords may have borne that name at that time. He distinguished himself in the struggle against the Saxon invaders.

Guinevere
Wife of Arthur, queen Guinevere committed adultery by succumbing to the advances of Mordred, usurper of the throne of his uncle, Arthur.

Merlin
The magician Merlin presided over the birth of Arthur. He enabled the construction of Stonehenge by using magic to move the stones of the giants of Ireland. Geoffrey of Monmouth relates his prophecies in the *History of the Kings of Britain* and develops them in *The Life of Merlin*.

Morgane
The fairy Morgane is one of the nine sisters on the island of fruits, Avalon. She appears in *The Life of Merlin*, a text published in 1148. Geoffrey tells us that she tended to the mortally wounded Arthur after the battle of Camblan against the troops of his rival Mordred.

Samson
Samson appears three times in the *History of the Kings of Britain*. When Merlin built Stonehenge, Aurèle was crowned king and gave Samson the archbishopric of York in England. Later, when visiting

York, King Arthur noted that the venerable archbishop Samson and all the other priests had been chased away by the Saxon invader. Finally Geoffrey of Monmouth cites Saint Samson again, this time as the archbishop of Dol, in the context of a redistribution of benefices ordered by Arthur.

Kay (or Keu)
Kay is the seneschal of Arthur. He appears in many later texts, at the king's side and often accompanied by Gawain. (For example, in Chrétien de Troyes' *Lancelot or the Knight of the Cart* and *Yvain, the Knight of the Lion*.)

Yvain
Son of king Urien.

Gawain (Gauvain)
Gawain, whose death Geoffrey records during the struggles against Mordred's troops, is one of the most famous knights of the Round Table. Like Mordred the nephew of Arthur, Gawain always stays faithful to the king. He is present in many later Arthurian texts.

Calibrun, forged on the Island of Avalon
Caliburn, later called Excalibur, is the sword of King Arthur. Forged by fairies from the magical island of Avalon, Caliburn performed veritable miracles, with the aid of God, according to Geoffrey's account.

When Geoffrey evokes the Pays de Dol

Geoffrey of Monmouth was inspired by the Pays de Dol, home of his ancestors, especially as cultural exchanges between the priories in Dol's territory (L'Abbaye-sous-Dol, Brégain) and the priory of Saint Florent in Monmouth, were maintained up to the time when the Arthurian legends were written down.

Near La Boussac the tower of the priory of Brégain still exists (private property, notopen for visits), topped by an oratory with a magnificent view over Mont Dol and neighbouring Mont-St-Michel.

In his *History of the Kings of Britain*, Geoffrey of Monmouth imagines Arthur going to Mont St-Michel (which the cleric notes by name), to rescue Helen, the niece of the king of Armorica, held prisoner by a giant.

This adventure is worth relating, especially as it gives a glimpse of Geoffrey's style.

Brégain – current state

Sunset over Tombelaine, with Mont St Michel to the left

Arthur at Mont St-Michel
by Geoffrey of Monmouth

Arthur heard that a giant of extraordinary size had arrived from Spain and abducted Helen, niece of Duke Hoel from her guardians, and then fled with her to the summit of a hill today called Mont St-Michel; two knights had chased the giant but could do nothing against him.

The following night, at the second hour, Arthur brought with him his seneschal Kay and his cup-bearer Bedevere. They had left their tents without telling their other companions and taken the path to Mont St-Michel. Arthur was so courageous that he did not think it worth advancing at the head of his army to confront monsters of this sort because not only did he feel strong enough to destroy them alone, but he also inspired his men by acting in this way.

When they came near the hill they saw a log fire on the summit and another on a smaller prominence a little distance from the first. Not knowing immediately in which of the two locations the giant actually was, they sent Bedevere on reconnaissance. He discovered a small boat in which he could sail towards the less high point, which was otherwise inaccessible because it gave straight into the sea. When he began the ascent, Bedevere heard, a woman's cries of lamentation coming from above, which terrified him at the time because he did not know if the monster was there. He also saw a recently erected tomb and beside it an old woman crying and groaning. When she saw Bedevere, she stopped crying at once and spoke to him as follows:

"O unfortunate man, what ill-chance brings you to this place? I pity you, I pity you because this abominable monster will destroy the flower of your youth this very night. The most gruesome giant - may his name be cursed - is on his way. It is he who brought the duke's niece here onto this mountain, with me, her nurse, and I have just buried her with my own hands."

Touched as deeply as a human being can be, Bedevere soothed the old woman with gentle words, then, having promised her the comfort of swift aid, he returned to Arthur and reported all he had discovered.

Arthur deplored the ill luck of the young woman and gave the order to his companions to let him attack the monster single-handed, whilst keeping themselves ready in case of need to lend him support and make a courageous attack. So they made their way towards the highest of the mountains, leaving their horses with the squires and began the climb, with Arthur at their head. The monster was keeping close to the fire, his mouth smeared with the blood of half-eaten pigs. He had swallowed some raw and was roasting the rest on skewers placed on the embers. As soon as he saw our heroes, who had taken him unawares, he rushed to grab his club, which two young men were trying to lift from the earth. The king drew his sword from its sheath, held his shield in front of him and rushed forward as quickly as possible to pre-empt the giant and stop him getting his club. But the giant, clearly understanding Arthur's intentions, had already got hold of it and struck the shield of the king with such immense force that the blow echoed all around: the whole coast resounded and Arthur's ears were completely deafened.

Immediately, enflamed by violent rage, the king brandished his sword at the giant's forehead, where he inflicted a wound which was not fatal, but caused blood to flow over his face and eyes, making him blind. In fact the giant had parried the blow with his club, so protecting his forehead from a deathly wound. Blinded by the flow of blood, he got up very quickly and like a wild boar which hurls itself on the hunter despite the hunting spear, so he rushed at the king and his sword, then seizing his opponent he forced him to his knees on the earth. Drawing on all his resources, Arthur disengaged himself quickly, and swift as lightning he struck the monster violently with his sword, first on one side then the other, not ceasing until he had inflicted a mortal wound, splitting his opponent's skull where it protects the brain. The horrible creature gave a great cry and, like an oak uprooted by powerful winds, he fell with a terrible crash.

At that moment when day chases away the night, our three victorious heroes returned to their tents with the head of the giant; all the men rushed up to admire it and heaped praise on the man who had liberated the area from such a monster. Saddened by the fate of his niece, Hoel gave an order to build a basilica on the spot where her corpse lay, on the mount which, in memory of the tomb of the young girl, carries to this day the name 'Helen's Tomb'.

Geoffrey of Monmouth was very well informed about the reigon of Dol and the Bay of Mont-St-Michel when he evoked 'a fire burning on the summit and another smaller one a short distance from the first'. That is a precise description of the scene, with the Mont of the Archangel and just to the north the little islet of Tombelaine. The word play of Tombelaine and Helen's tomb was taken up by the troubadours, like Wace who translated Geoffrey of Monmouth into French in the 12th century, even if the real etymology of the place is something quite different – the Romanesque context makes this inevitable.

Clearly this same islet of Tombelaine gave Geoffrey the idea of the island of nine fairies in the *Life of Merlin*. This account tells us of nine sisters occupying the island of fruits or the blessed isle (Avalon) where one lives for a hundred years or more. It is there that King Arthur would be cared for after his final wound; the eldest of the sisters, Morgane, knew the art of healing with plants. In what we call the *Matière de Bretagne*, which inspired Geoffrey of Monmouth, there is a clear allusion to the Druidesses of Tombelaine, nine in number. We will read later in this context the analysis of historian Marc Decenneux in *Mont-Saint-Michel, Histoire d'un mythe* (Editions Ouest-France 1997).

Samson, a contemporary of Arthur

Let us return to the presence of Saint Samson, bishop of Dol-de-Bretagne, in Geoffrey's account. Samson and Arthur were contemporaries. It appears that this element has not received sufficient attention up until now; because if the historicity of Arthur is far from proved, and if Guinevere, Merlin and Gawain are imaginary figures, there is one person – and only one – attested by historians: Samson. The bishop of Dol is mentioned at the Council of Paris in 557, and his existence is also well attested, unlike a lot of Breton saints, whose Lives (Vitae in Latin) are sometimes nothing more than romance. Born in Wales about 480, Saint Samson died in Dol in 565. Geoffrey of Monmouth is right to make him a contemporary of Arthur, dead in 542.

Once again, the area of Dol-Combourg appears as an essential reference in the writing of Arthurian tales.

The Grail at Dol-de-Bretagne: a relic

During the lifetime of Geoffrey of Monmouth, a singular legend was created in Brittany: it is recorded for us by Baudry de Bourgueil, archbishop of Dol (born about 1045, d.1130) in his *Chronique de Dol*.

Baudry wrote:

"The sanctity of the man, Saint Budoc, was shown by the fact he brought back a precious gift from the sacred city of Jerusalem: that is to say, a cup and platter which Our Lord used at the Last Supper with his disciples". This is the first mention of the Grail in the West, in the geographical context of the Arthurian tales.

Budoc was the third bishop of Dol, after Saint Samson and Saint Magloire. He lived in the 6th century, that of Arthur and Merlin, and was of Irish or Welsh origin. He would have installed the cup of the Last Supper of Jesus before the Passion, (the cup which would become the Grail) at Dol-de-Bretagne.

The cathedral of Dol (13th century)

It is not for us to judge the credibility of this transfer. Let us just say that Baudry, when he wrote the *Chronique de Dol* existed in a period of history when the fabrication of relics was commonplace in the West. The archbishop of Dol had a lot to gain in suggesting the presence of the Pascal Cup in the cathedral (Romanesque at that time) of this small Breton city.

We will see what happened later on: to continue, Baudry de Bourgueil made contact with the monks of Fécamp who possessed another celebrated relic, still honoured in our own time, a vial containing the Sacred Blood of Jesus Christ. The cup of the Last Supper associated with blood of our saviour together forged the Christian vision of the holy Grail. Remember for the moment this origin in Dol, once again involved in the legend from which the troubadours who wrote the Arthurian cycle drew their material.

Combourg

1155: Wace translates Geoffrey of Monmouth …. and introduces Brocéliande

In 1155, the same year in which Geoffrey died, the Norman clerk Wace finished the translation of the *History of the Kings of Britain* into French verse in the *Roman de Brut*, which naturally has the same characters. Ten years later, Wace wrote the *Roman de Rou*, a history of the duchy of Normandy. It is here that the miraculous spring of Barenton and the legendary forest of Brocéliande appeared. Here is the original text:

E li sire i vint de Dinan,	Here came the lord of Dinan
e Raol i vint de Gael,	and Raoul de Gael, several Bretons
e maint Breton de maint chastel,	coming from several castles,
e cil devers Brecheliant	and also from Brocéliande
donc Breton vont sovent fablant,	which the Bretons often speak of
une forest mult longue e lee	in stories, A large, wide forest,
qui en Bretaigne est mult loee.	Which is well-known in Brittany.

Wace does not give a precise location for the forest of Brocéliande, a site which has been the cause of much speculation over the centuries. We know only that here it is in Armorican Brittany and that it is close to, but not to be confused with the lands of Dinan and Gael-Monfort.

A modern translation would be:

Brocéliande, which the Bretons often speak of in stories,
A large, wide forest,
Which is well-known in Brittany.

This forest "which the Bretons often speak of in stories" is described by a contemporary of Wace, Guillaume de Saint-Pair, who calls it Quokelunde in the *Roman du Mont Saint Michel*. The forest of Quokelunde, which was much talked of in the wider world, spreads from east to west, from Avranches to Alet (today St-Malo). It includes the state-owned forests which still today border the territory of Dol-Combourg.

Last quarter of the 12th century, beginning of the 13th:
Percival and Lancelot-du-Lac

At the end of the 12th century and beginning of the next, the Arthurian myth was completed by troubadours writing in the romance language of Old French: Chrétien de Troyes, Robert de Boron and the anonymous author(s) of *Lancelot en Prose* (also called *Lancelot-Grall*).

To complete the list of earlier protagonists, two major new characters appeared: Percival and Lancelot.

Percival appeared in the unfinished eponymous story by Chrétien de Troyes, *Perceval ou le conte du Graal*. Here it is he who brings the quest to an end. We should note that later accounts give this supreme honour to Galahad, son of Lancelot.

According to Chrétien de Troyes the cup of the Grail contains a host, which Robert de Boron makes the container of the blood of the Passion.

You will find in the appendix a note relating to Mont Dol, situated a few kilometres north of the cathedral of Saint Samson. Many analogies link this with Mont Doloureuse of the Arthurian legend, scene of Percival's final stage before he discovers the Grail. Besides, even if the true etymology of Dol de Bretagne is unconnected, the troubadours were able to exploit the double meaning: in Old French Mont Dol means the hill of pain.

Lancelot-du-lac is best known to us from *Lancelot en Prose*, from the early 13th century. Chrétien de Troyes however devoted a story to him, *Lancelot ou le Chevalier de la Charette (Lancelot or the Knight of the Cart)*, which tells us of the impossible love of the hero for Queen Guinivere, wife of Arthur, and indicates that the knight was brought up by a fairy, without saying more.

It was necessary to wait for *Lancelot-Grall* to make all clear.

While the Knights of the Round Table are most often Welsh or English, Lancelot is an exception: he was born in Little Britain (Brittany), or Armorican Brittany in French; more precisely, in the Marches of Brittany.

Lancelot en Prose is very explicit, beginning with these words: "There was once in the Marches of Gaul and Brittany..." and the anonymous author adds, regarding the fairy Viviane who brought up Lancelot: "There was in the Marches of Brittany a young woman of very great beauty, who was called Ninienne (Viviane). Merlin fell in love with her and was often with her day and night".

Lancelot's father, Ban de Benoic, died whilst watching the destruction of his château by fire from a hill-top near Lac de Diane which was in the care of the fairy Viviane, the Lady of the Lake. The story tells that this prominence was three leagues, that is to say 12kms, from the burning château of Ban. Viviane took Lancelot in and brought him up, before taking him across the channel to the court of King Arthur.

The 13th century text gives us a very valuable indication for pinpointing the sites concerned: the blazon of Lancelot, which constitutes a unique and well-known signature in the medieval world. The knight's shield is *argent* (white) with three bands of *gueles* (red). Now this coat-of-arms exists in reality and belongs in fact to one of the great families of the Marches of Brittany, who distinguished themselves at the time of the Crusades: the Coëtquen family. Their territory was situated between Combourg and Dinan. On the cover of this book you can see a miniature of the 15th century showing Lancelot bearing these arms of the Coëtquen family, with the Château de Combourg in the centre, and on the right the blazon painted on the ceiling of the hall in this fortress: the Coëtquen family owned the Château de Combourg for several centuries.

The *motte* of Ban still exists today in the forest of Coëtquen. It can be found, as the story says, 12km from the hill named Landes de Riniac, which overlooks Lake Tranquil dear to the writer Chateaubriand, at the foot of the medieval fortress of Combourg. The conformity of these actual places with those in the romance is unsettling. The feudal motte of Coëtquen family was burnt twice during the Viking invasions.

The Druids' Stones on the Landes de Riniac

And so we believe that the Lac de Diane of the Arthurian cycle is that of Combourg, nestled in the hollow of a valley. One must note that the *Lancelot-Graal* never places this lake in the forest of Brocéliande, but in a smaller wooded place named the Bois-en-Val (*Lancelot en Prose*, early 13th century).

Fougères and Vitré,
in the Marches of Brittany

And Brocéliande?

The localisation of the mythical forest of Brocéliande never ceases to occupy the pens of writers of varying degrees of qualification. The Fontaine de Barenton is found there, but there's no shortage of springs in Brittany and each Brocéliande (Breton or Norman) has its Barenton! At the beginning of the 19th century, this forest was said to be situated near Quintin in the department of Côtes d'Armor. This location, today no longer seriously considered, had the merit of consisting of forested uplands near to the sea. For the Arthurian literature from the earliest time is clear: Brocéliande is near the sea and one has only to read the Welsh tale *Owein* or *Le Conte de la Dame et la Fontaine* to be convinced of this. This text draws on the same sources and completes the account of Chrétien de Troyes, *Yvain, Le Chevalier au Lion (Yvain, the Knight of the Lion)*.

To find the spring of Barenton, the hero (Yvain/Owein) goes near to the sea: "So I arrived in a great field, at the end of which I could see a shining château, situated near the ocean". He stays the night there, then finds the spring:

"The next morning, when the young girls had prepared Owein's horse, he got as far as the forest clearing where he met a black knight. Owein found his size was greater than Kynon had said. He asked the man the way and the other showed it to him. Owein followed the route Kynon had taken, right up to the green tree. There he saw the spring with the slab and basin. Owen took the basin and used it to pour water onto the slab. Then the thunder came and after the thunder, hail, in much greater force than Kynon had said."

Quintin is a credible location of Brocéliande because it is not far from the sea, but this attribution makes little sense in the distance which separates the forest of Lorge (near Quintin) from the Marches of Brittany, where the action takes place.

Paimpont

Another attempt at fixing the location was also made in the first half of the 19th century. Maître Poignant, a judge at Montfort near Paimpont, opted for this forest in central Brittany. The poet Blanchard de la Musse put together the pieces for him.

The story is well-known, thanks to Marcel Calvez, who submitted a thesis to the University of Paris X in 1984. In this the conditions of the assimilation of Paimpont to the adventure-filled forest of the romances of the Round Table are considered.

The sham is exposed:

There is a copy of this thesis in university library of Rennes 1 which we were able to consult. Let us explain at once that it is a doctoral thesis of the third cycle in sociology supported before the group of sociological researchers of CNRS at Nanterre, in a context guaranteeing a perfectly rigorous scientific method of the study. The result confirms our gravest doubts about Paimpont and Brocéliande.

In 1812, when the general public were largely ignorant of the Arthurian romances, a work appeared which made them fashionable again: *The Knights of the Round Table*, a poem in 20 chants, 'drawn from the old story-tellers'. The author, Creuzé de Lesser, notably evoked the Valley of No Return. Here the fairy Morgane kept unfaithful lovers prisoner until they were rescued by Lancelot. The success of the book was great and the chivalry of the Grail made a comeback.

In 1824, Blanchard de la Musse cleverly took possession of the legend. This native of Montfort-sur-Meu, a town bordering the forest of Paimpont, wrote: "the little river flowing from this place is called Mell-Aon. It is made famous by the ninth chant of the poem of the Round Table under the allegorical name of old

MELIADUS which must be followed along the Valley of No Return as far as its source in the forest of Brécilien, to find the two tombs of Merlin and his lady Viviane." With a well-merited irony, Marcel Calvez remarks in his thesis: "we simply note that the author has made a significant error regarding Méladius seeing that the name designates not a river but one of the knights who tried the adventure of the Valley of No Return." But with what consequence! The legend of Paimpont was in construction from then onwards, and not without unforeseen developments.

Blanchard de la Musse had found his Valley of No Return: it only remained to round off this marvellous theory. We will look for the tomb of Merlin at the sources of the Mel. The book of Creusé de Lesser conforms to the legend: the tomb of Merlin is a grotto which Gawain will discover; a 'cave' in which the fairy Viviane imprisoned the sorcerer by magic. "These caves resounded with a terrible sound and the hero's hair stood on end" wrote our poet. His style may not revolutionize French literature, but at least we must acknowledge his loyalty to the legends of the Round Table (*Lancelot en Prose*, 13th century). The tomb of Merlin is a cave.
Yes, but the difficulty is that there are no caves in the forest of Paimpont. No problem! Blanchard de la Musse has no intention of stopping on his course and finds a ruined megalithic at the source of the Mel, a large stone which will make an excellent tomb for the magician. Tourist promotion may now begin.

A knight becomes a river, a cave is changed into a stone... And what follows shows what a little bit of romantic imagination can do. The Valley of No Return will have its own twists and turns; the construction of a factory ruined the beauty of the scene. It was necessary to move the legendary site from the east (where the sources of the Mell are) to the west of the forest of Paimpont, where it is now designated. But at this level this is no more than a slight incoherence. The tomb of Merlin stayed where it was, and was therefore no longer tied to the geography of the Valley of No Return.

Marcel Calvez explains: "The first mention of a localization (of the Valley of No Return) in the place when it now lies is in a work by Cayot-Delandre (1847)". It is true that the new proposed site, situated in the commune of Tréhorenteuc, is an idyllic spot, so much so that it seduced Abbé Gillard, the priest in charge of the parish, in the 20th century. He was more attracted by the esotericism and mystery of the Grail than by the dogma of the church, something which attracted the wrath of his superiors, as the good priest completely transformed the decoration of the parish church to create a temple dedicated to the Grail quest. Thus was the construction of the legend in the forest of Paimpont created in the 19th and 20th century.

For Chateaubriand, Brocéliande was at Combourg and Dol

Far from the ocean, far from the Marches of Brittany, the hypothesis of the forest of Paimpont as Brocéliande cannot stand against a rigorous scrutiny of the sources.

In the end, the only localization conforming to the accounts of the 12th and 13th centuries (*Lancelot en Prose*, Anonymous, Guillaume de Saint-Pair) seems to us to be that expressed by the author François-René de Chateaubriand, whose adolescent years passed at the Château de Combourg (and childhood at college in Dol), an account made more credible by a perfect knowledge of the actual places, and Breton history and culture.

Chateaubriand wrote:

"From the 12th century, the cantons of Fougères, Rennes, Bécherel, Dinan, St Malo and Dol were occupied by the forest of Brechéliant (*Memoires d'Outre Tomb*).

And the great Breton writer adds: "I take Brechéliant for Bécherel, near Combourg (*Essay on English Lierature*).

This forested area is still widely present today: In a radius of 17km around Combourg, we have calculated more than 5000 hectares of woods and forests, enough to grant the official appellation '*station verte*' (Green Environment) to the town.

To the north of Combourg: the state-owned forest covers more than 2000 hectares, divided into three zones:

The forests of Villecartier (979 hectares), Mesnil (592 hectares) and Coëtquen (557 hectares).

Ruins of the Château of Coëtquen (not open for visits)

In these well-maintained forests enjoying free access, a visitor can discover the traces of another magical time. Around these tree-lined routes, he will find the feudal *motte* of Lancelot, a megalithic covered passage grave called the Fairies' House, a Roman military borne and many other curiosities with the flavour of legend.

Dol-Combourg and the legend of the Grail

The legend of King Arthur was created in the 12th century on the basis of Celtic traditions from Wales and those of Armorica called the *Matière de Bretagne*. With *History of the Kings of Britain*, Geoffrey of Monmouth created the seminal text in about 1135, the true prototype of Arthurian tales, from which arose Arthur, Guinevere, Merlin, Gawain and Morgan Le Fey. The legend of the Grail also developed in the 12th century. We shall discover the important role played by the seigneury of Dol-Combourg, situated in the Marches of Brittany.

In the 11th century, Caradoc de la Boussac (a place near Dol) swore fealty to Rivallon of Dol, lord of Combourg. These two families (whose family tree we shall present in a simplified form) played a part in the spread of a local legend exploited by Geoffrey of Monmouth in the next century:

- Caradoc first of all, whose sons received the lordship of Monmouth, and who was more than likely the ancestor of Geoffrey of Monmouth.

- Secondly Rivallon, whose eldest son became abbot of Saint-Florent-de-Saumur. Under his initiative three priories subject to this Benedictine abbey were founded, including Saint Florent of Monmouth. From one priory to another, the Celtic legend did the rounds.

Lastly, we shall see how an account emanating from Baudry, archbishop of Dol, prefigures the myth of the Christian Grail.

From Dol-Combourg to Monmouth

The *Lancelot-Graal* or *Lancelot en Prose*, produced at the beginning of the 13th century, gave the birthplace of the knight as in the '*marches of Gaul and Little Britain*'. It was there that

Lancelot-du-Lac would be welcomed by the fairy Viviane, the Lady of the Lake, with whom Merlin would fall in love. It is there too that our account begins. In the Marches of Brittany a defensive line of castles was erected, which to the east separated Brittany from French territory, linking Dol-de-Bretagne to Clisson by way of Combourg, Fougères and Vitré, to cite only the most famous fortresses. We are concerned with the seigneury of Dol-Combourg, the northern part of the Marches which borders the 'Cornish Sea' important in the Arthurian tales: the Channel.

In the 11th century, the same family ruled at Dol and Combour (today Combourg), two small towns 15km apart. Dol was then a Breton archbishopric, the most important religious place in an independent Brittany. Ginguené was archbishop there in 1040, while his young brother Rivallon-de-Dol, lord of Combourg, was responsible for defending the seigneury. In 1064 Rivallon headed a league against the duke of Brittany, Conan II, who was besieging the castle at Dol. This historic episode features on the famous Bayeux Tapestry: one can see the troops of William (later the Conqueror), Duke of Normandy, whom Rivallon had asked for help, putting Conan's men to flight at Dol. Two years later, at the time of the Battle of Hastings in 1066, various Breton lords would accompany Duke William in his conquest of England. Among these were Guihénoc of Dol and his brother Baderon de La Boussac, both belonging to the seigneury of Dol-Combourg.

Victorious and now king of England, William the Conqueror distributed lands, including some to the minor Armorican nobility. So in 1076 Guihénoc de Dol, son of Caradoc de La Boussac, subject to Dol-Combourg, received the castle of Monmouth in Wales. There he founded a priory dependent on the Benedictine abbey of Saint-Florent de Saumur. To understand why, we must return for a moment to the seigneury of Dol-Combourg.

Rivallon de Dol, lord of Combourg, had three sons, the eldest of whom, Guillaume, became abbot of Saint-Florent de Saumur. The second son, Jean, was in turn lord of Combourg and archbishop of Dol. Finally Gilduin was chosen archbishop of Dol but refused the position, through humility it is said. The relics of Gilduin, who was made a saint, are still today honoured in the church of Combourg and the chapel of the château, the cathedral at Dol and Saint-Pierre in Chartres.

At the instigation of Guillaume de Dol, his brother Jean created a priory depending on Saint-Florent de Saumur in about 1070: the Abbaye-sous-Dol. Likewise, at La Boussac near Dol, the Baderon established the priory of Brégain, which was also dependent on Saint-Florent-les-Saumur.

In this context, at Monmouth, Guihénoc de Dol quite naturally looked to the abbey of Saint-Florent-les-Saumur for creating a priory. Once he became a monk, he *assured a hold over the land by the arrival of dependants originally from the parishes of Epiniac and La Boussac near Dol'.*[1]

At the beginning of the 12th century, the castle of Monmouth and the priory remained under the control of the Breton family: we know that Baderon of Monmouth, born about 1100, succeeded his father William Fitzbaderon in 1125 and became lord of Monmouth. It is more than likely – indeed, established – that Geoffrey of Monmouth, with an Armorican first name and also born about 1100, belonged to the same family. His pen would write the first account of the Arthurian cycle.

History of the Kings of Britain

In the 12th century, Geoffrey of Monmouth wrote the first instalment of the Arthurian legend, *History of the Kings of Britain* (meaning Great Britain, about 1135-1138) and the *Life of Merlin*, written in 1148.

For the first time the essential elements of the Arthurian myth were assembled, except for the Grail. Geoffrey of Monmouth drew on various ancient texts and certain oral traditions from Wales and from Armorica, the *Matière de Bretagne*. So the following stories are told:

- The birth of Arthur, illegitimate son of the king Uther Pendragon. The magician Merlin gave Uther the appearance of the husband of the woman he coveted, the mother of Arthur. The future king was thus conceived in adultery at Tintagel (Cornwall).

- The death of Arthur, in the year 540: Merlin transported the mortally wounded king to the Isle of Avalon, where he was cared for by Morgan le Fey.

- The sword of Arthur, Caliburn (which became Escalibor, Excalibur), forged on the Isle of Avalon.

- Queen Guinevere, and her infidelity.

- The most valorous Gawain, who in later accounts would be one of the best knights of the Round Table

- The magic of Merlin, which helped the construction of Stonehenge.

Geoffrey of Monmouth, surrounded by clerks originally from the seignury of Dol-Combourg, did not forget his Armorican origins. So Merlin is akin to an historical and very real individual, Samson, the first archbishop of Dol-de-Bretagne (died at Dol about 565, and thus a contemporary of the supposed Arthurian era). He whom the Armorican Bretons call Saint Samson appears in chapters 130, 151 and 157 of the *History of the Kings of Britain*. The cathedral at Dol is dedicated to him.

The tower of the priory of Brégain near Dol (now private property) today offers a magnificent view of Mont Dol, the sea and, in clear weather, Mont St Michel 18 km away. Geoffrey knew the latter's legend well (remember that the priories of Brégain and Monmouth were linked when he wrote the *History of the Kings of Britain*). Geoffrey of Monmouth relates the combat between Arthur and a giant (Chapter 165) on the summit of Mont St Michel. The giant had seized Helen, niece of the duke of Armorica, Hoel. Arthur arrived too late to save Helen, but killed the giant. Medieval chronicles accept the fanciful etymology of the islet situated north of Mont St Michel: *tombelaine* for 'Helen's tomb'. The *Life of St Samson* (7th century) describes the forest witch and her eight sisters who were to inspire the nine Druidesses of Tombelaine. These seminal legends were used by Geoffrey of Monmouth in his *Life of Merlin*, when the magician escorts the dying Arthur to the Isle of Avalon: the king was cared for there by Morgan Le Fey and her eight sisters.[2]

From the seigneury of Dol-Combourg to Monmouth, the *matière de Bretagne* largely inspired Geoffrey's account. Only the Grail is needed to reconstruct the Arthurian epoch.

The Grail makes its appearance at Dol

To understand how the Grail was introduced into the Arthurian legend, we must return to the seigneury of Dol-Combourg, at the beginning of the 12th century. But what Grail are we speaking of?

In his unfinished romance *Perceval or the Story of the Grail*, Chrétien de Troyes evokes a chalice. This text, written between 1180 and 1190 tells us of Perceval's vision: a grail in gold, accompanied by a silver platter and a bloodied lance. The Christian symbolism makes it clear that we are speaking of the Passion. There the grail contained nothing but a single wafer, but the blood of Christ was associated with it[3].

Ten years later, Robert de Boron fixed the Christian context: after the Passion, the blood of Christ was collected by Joseph of Arimathea (companion of Nicodeme, according to John's gospel) in the chalice used by Jesus during the Last Supper with his disciples.

Later, other versions developed: for the German poet Wolfram von Eschenbach, the Grail was a stone fallen from heaven. One can mention the emerald on the forehead of Lucifer. Some modern commentators equate the Grail with the magic cauldron of the Celts, when it is not the cornucopia of the ancient Greeks.

We prefer to stick with the first vision of Chrétien des Troyes and Robert de Boron, that of the **Sacred Chalice**.

But it is at Dol, nearly a century before *Joseph or the Story of the Grail* by Robert de Boron that we find the first mention of the Sacred Chalice recorded in the west.

Jean, son of Rivallon, lord of Combourg and archbishop of Dol, died in 1092 after founding the Abbey-below-Dol, in actual fact a priory depending on Saint-Florent-de-Saumur. At the same period and near Saumur, in 1089, a key figure in the Arthurian cycle became abbot: Baudry de Bourgeuil (1046-1130). Consequently, it is not surprising to see him obtain in 1107 the coveted position of archbishop of Dol. Baudry wrote the **Chronicle of Dol**, evoking his predecessors, including Budoc (6th century), third bishop of Dol, following Saint Samson and Magloire:

"Such was the saintliness of this man, Saint Budoc, attested by the precious gift he brought from the sacred city of Jerusalem: that is to say, the cup and the platter which our Lord used during the Last Supper which he took with his disciples"[4].

And so, according to Baudry, the archbishop of Dol, the Sacred Chalice travelled from Jerusalem to the little Breton town in the 6th century. It should be noted that the platter from the Last Supper accompanied the cup, a fact which recalls the text of Chrétien de Troyes describing the silver platter which followed the Grail.

As Baudry was not a troubadour, the reason for his account must be posed. It is true that in the west the 12th century saw the discovery of relics which attracted numerous pilgrims and contributed to the financing of basilicas, cathedrals and monasteries of all kinds. But the archbishop of Dol goes further, taking interest in another potential relic: the Sacred Blood of Fécamp. About 1120, Baudry de Bourgueil wrote to the monks at Fécamp:

"Your monastery glories in possessing the blood of Our Lord, Jesus Christ, buried by Nicodeme, as St John attests, the blood which he had taken from his body".[5]

So here are assembled in the first quarter of the 12th century and from the pen of the archbishop of Dol, all the elements which constitute the legend of the Grail: the transfer of the cup and the platter used at the Last Supper from Jerusalem to the west; the relic of the Sacred Blood gathered by Nicodeme and Joseph of Arimathea. So Baudry precedes the Christian Grail of Robert de Boron by nearly a century.

The prelate of Dol would visit England. He died in January 1130, a few years before the edition of the *History of the Kings of England* by Geoffrey of Monmouth. At this time the relic of the Precious Blood was nothing more than a legend at Fécamp. Its discovery merits an explanation. Martin Aurell, a great specialist in the Arthurian Cycle and professor of medieval history at the University of Potiers, describes the conditions:

"In July 1171, the abbot Henri de Sully, second cousin of King Henry II (of England) discovered this relic in a column of the abbatial church in the course of restoration work after a fire. Then the legend goes that it had formerly been hidden there by duke Richard 1st (942-996) to prevent its profanation".[5]

The same author adds that Henri de Sully, once he became abbot of Glastonbury, discovered the tombs of King Arthur and Queen Guinevere:

"More prosaically, the remains of Arthur and Guinevere attracted visitors and alms to Glastonbury, money necessary for the reconstruction of the monastery which had been destroyed by fire in 1184. Henri de Sully, named its head by his cousin Richard the Lionheart in September 1189, was accustomed to the discovery of relics. Twenty years earlier he proceeded in identical circumstances to discover the Sacred Blood at Fécamp, also a monastery harmed by fire where he was abbot".[6]

At Glastonbury the legend of the Grail thus coincides with the epoch of King Arthur. There's nothing astonishing in that when one knows that Geoffrey of Monmouth was familiar with Oxford and Glastonbury. So the way was opened for the writing of the Arthurian tales. Chrétien de Troyes, Wace, Robert de Boron and their successors owed much to this legend born at least partly with the seigneury of Dol-Combourg.

1. In this context, see Hubert Guillotel, A Breton family in service of the Conqueror : the Baderon. Paris, PUF, 1976.

2. Marc Déceneux, Mont Saint-Michel, Histoire d'un mythe (History of a Myth). Editions Ouest-France, 1997. Page 108 : *Let us return for a precise analysis of the theme to the magicians of the island of Sein: these creatures from the other-world, presented as real beings by the un-nuanced rationalism of a Latin author, are close in medieval Welsh literature to the nine witches of the Mabinogion tale of Peredur ap Evrawc and, in Armorican texts of the Late Middle Age, to the forest witch and her eight sisters described in the Life of Saint Samson (7th century). But even more than these hideous, fearful and demonized creatures, the priestesses of Sein resemble the nine fairies, Morgan and her sisters, who, according to Geoffrey of Monmouth in the Life of Merlin, reign over the enchanted Isle of Avalon where Arthur was transported after being wounded at the battle of Camlann.*

3 Chrétien de Troyes, Perceval or the Story of the Grail. From the modern French translation by Jean-Pierre Foucher and André Ortais, published by Gallimard:

As they talked of this and that, a servant came from the chamber, carrying a shining spear, grasping it in the middle. He passed by the fire and those who were sitting there. A drop of blood flowed from the iron point of the spear and this crimson drop ran onto the hand of the valet. The younq host saw this wonder and had to control himself so as not to ask what it meant.

Then he remembered the words of his mentor in chivalry. Hadn't he taught him not to speak too much? To pose the question was base behaviour. He said not a word.

Then two servants came holding golden candelabras finished in niello. The servants who carried these candelabras were very handsome. Each candelabra contained ten blazing candles to say the least. A very beautiful young woman, slender and well turned-out, who accompanied the servants, held the grail between her hands. When she had entered the room with the Grail, so great a light appeared that the candles lost their brilliance like stars when the sun or moon rise. Behind her followed another maiden who carried a silver dish. The Grail which preceded her was made of the purest gold. It was studded with precious stones of many kinds, the richest and most valuable to be found by sea or land.

4. Original text in Latin : *Quantae vero sanctitatis fuerit vir iste sanctus Budocus, pretiosa munera quae secum de sancta civitate detulit Jérusalem, scutella scilicet et scutellus quibus Dominus usus est in ultima Coena quam cum discipulis suis fecit testantur.*

Baudry de Bourgueil, Chronique de Dol. Manuscript 14617 in the Bibliothèque Nationale de France. *Acta Sanctorum Ordinis Sancti Benedicti Saec. I, pages 223-225.*

5. Martin Aurell, The Legend of King Arthur, Perrin, Paris 2007. Pages 474 and 475.

6. Martin Aurell, op.cit. pages 198 and 199.

APPENDIX 1
Notes on Mont Dol and Combourg

These two notes are the fruit of an earlier book. They are taken from a collective work (published in 2011 by Charles Corlet Editions) presented under the direction of Dr Georges Bertin: *Le Nouveau Guide Arthurien Normandie-Maine, la route arthurienne aux Marches de Gaule et de Petite Bretagne* (The New Arthurian Guide to Normandy-Maine; an Arthurian route through the Marches of Gaul and Brittany). These two notes are our contribution to this work.

It should be noted that Georges Bertin, who supervised the work, is one of the greatest French specialists of the legend of King Arthur and the Holy Grail. He is a Doctor of Sciences of Education authorized to direct sociological research, as in his books on the Arthurian cycle.

MONT-DOL

The history of Mont Dol is almost inseparable from that of Mont St Michel. The sacred mountain, as Chateaubriand liked to call it, would become an essential stopping-point for Percival at the end of his quest in the romances of the Grail. At 20km west of the hill of the archangel, this land of legends is the Mont Doloreux of the Round Table cycle, a magnificent site, a natural viewpoint dominating the whole area.

Christianised in the 6th century by Saint Samson, who came from Wales, Mont Dol was one of the first Armorican sites dedicated to St Michael. The Welsh bishop overrode older pagan beliefs on the hill of Jupiter which was later to become Mont Dol, and Jupiter and Mithras were replaced in their solar roles by the archangel Michael. In 1158 the archbishop of Dol gave the chapel of St MIchel to the Benedictines. According to tradition, this was constructed on the base of a pagan temple to Diana, and probably using the same materials. Bulls and white stags were sacrificed to the goddess, and two taurobolic altars are confirmed at Mont Dol, serving the cults of Diana and Mithras in turn.

Immediately the history of Mont Dol chimes well in the ears of Arthurian enthusiasts. If Brocéliande is a forest near the sea of Cornouaille - what today is the Channel - this mythical territory stretches from Avranches to St Malo. The Norman and Breton forests on each side of the river Sélune provided material for the legendary world of the Round Table. In the 12th century Guillaume Saint-Pair named this forested area Quokelunde, the etymology of which is comparable to that of Brocéliande. It was there that Viviane, the Lady of Lake of Diana, took in Lancelot, there that the wizard Merlin met the fairy, sometimes taking the form of a white stag. Diana and the white stag, an animal which we have noted was sacrificed to her on Mont Dol, was an evident source of inspiration for the troubadours of the Arthurian Cycle.

The relationship between the site and the legends of the Round Table becomes crystal clear on reading Chrétien de Troyes' *Perceval*. This account tells how Merlin places a column and a cross on the summit of the hill destined to welcome the greatest knight in the world. Historically a Roman column Christianised in the 6th century is recorded on the summit of Mont Dol; today it stands in the parish church (open for visits). Percival tied up his horse there, received by the daughter of Merlin, the *Demoiselle du Grand Puits* or Damsel of the Great Wells. Another connection: a geological peculiarity causes a source to rise and a lake to form on the summit of the rocky prominence of Mont Dol. From there, Percival rejoined the Fisher King in the Land Laid Waste (*Terre Gâte*) on the banks of the Sélune, an impassable watercourse. On both banks, this river is edged with place-names from the Land Laid Waste of the Arthurian romances. Saint-Laurent-de-Terregatte and Saint-Aubin de Terregatte border the route of our hero, which takes him from Dol to the Fisher King and on as far as the Grail. Is this also the route followed by followed by Yvain, the Knight of the Lion, advancing right up to the sources of the Sélune at the *Fontaine de L'Air S'ouvre* near to Barenton in Normandy? It was at Mont-Dol that Viviane finally imprisoned Merlin in a cave, on the north flank of the hill (difficult access).

The cave on Mont Dol, Tomb of Merlin

The visitor should not leave Dol without a visit to the 13th century cathedral, and, on the route to Combourg, the wonderful *fontaine* (sacred spring) of Saint Samson at Carfantin, guarded by the *menhir* of the Champ Dolent. A story tells that this standing-stone of nearly 10m in height separated two brothers determined to kill each other: an Arthurian theme if ever there was one.

The *menhir* of Champ Dolent

COMBOURG

About 30km to the south-west of Mont St-Michel, the medieval fortress of Combourg (a feudal *motte* in the 11th century, fortified castle from the 13-15th centuries) is the heart of Romantic Brittany, immortalised by Chateaubriand. The Brittany of romance stories also: Geoffrey of Monmouth from the Baderon family, descendants of the seigneury of Dol-Combourg, laid the foundations of the Arthurian legend in the *Life of Merlin* and *History of the Kings of Britain*.

Like Passais in Normandy, this is frontier territory. The château, centrepiece of the defensive line of the Marches of Brittany, was originally intended as a protection for the cathedral of Dol. A weighty task! The archbishop Baudry de Bourgueil in his chronicle of Dol written at the beginning of the 12th century relates the visit of his 6th century predecessor Budoc to Jerusalem: "The sanctity of the man, Saint Budoc, was shown by the fact he brought back a precious gift from the sacred city of Jerusalem: that is to say, a cup and platter which Our Lord used at the Last Supper with his disciples".

The actual etymology of Combourg (valley-frontier) recalls that on both sides the river Sélune spreads into the territory of the Marches where Lancelot was one of the heroes.

François-René de Chateaubriand reveals in *Memoirs from beyond the Tomb*: "It is in the woods of Combourg that I became what I am." And the illustrious writer places the forest of Brocéliande, which reaches as far as the ocean, here. "Today the area preserves the tell-tale signs of its origin: interspersed with woody depressions, it has from afar the appearance of a forest, and recalls England. It was the home of fairies and you will see indeed how I met my sylph there", wrote Chateaubriand.

A visit to the chateau today begins in the hall where the ceiling is decorated with the blazons of illustrious families: Chateaubriand, of course, who saved the life of the king Saint Louis during the crusades, and his companions-in-arms, the Coëtquen and Lusignan families. Any visitor with a good knowledge of Arthurian iconography will not fail to spot that, unsurprisingly, the arms attributed to Percival are those of Lusignan, as well as that the blazon of Lancelot du Lac described in *Les Enfances* (13th century) - argent (white) with three bands of gueles (red) - are those of the Coëtquen, kin of Dol-Combourg: the valiant crusaders lending their arms to the mythical knights of the Grail. The analogy does not stop there, because the account of *Les Enfances* of Lancelot describes the journey from the fief of Coëtquen to the Château de Combourg very precisely. The geography, the distance of three leagues (12km) covered by the father of Lancelot fleeing his domain, the lake of Diana at the end, all fit very well indeed. "Finally he arrived with his escort beside a lake at the edge of the heath, at the foot of a height from which one could control the whole area" *Les Enfances* tells us. This height exists: it is a very remarkable site called the Landes de Riniac at 3km from Combourg and its '*Lac tranquille*'.

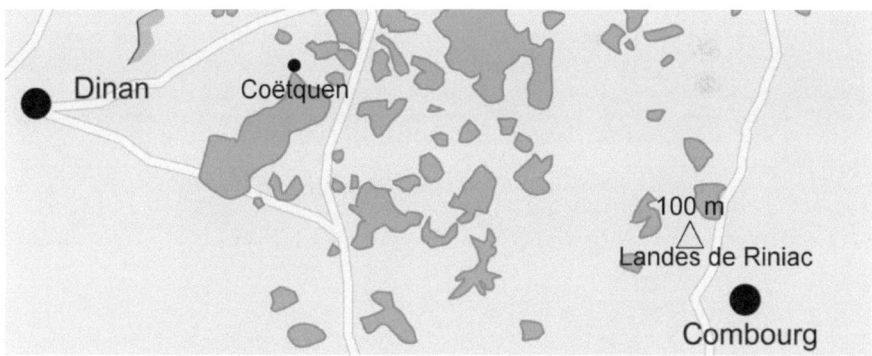

The anonymous author of *Les Enfances* also tells us that the Lady of the Lake is none other than Lilienne (Viviane), the fairy who stole the heart and the magical powers of Merlin, and kept him prisoner in the forest. In an etymological context, Ninienne could have given rise to Linienne, then Linon, name of the river feeding the Lake of Diana at Combourg. Yes, the Lady of *Lac de Diane* haunts these places, like the ghost with a wooden leg and accompanied by a black cat who lives inside the fortress. King Arthur, wounded in the thigh if one believe believes the Welsh tales, victoriously fought the Chapalu, a monstrous cat.

The Château de Combourg, home of the Lady of the Lake

APPENDIX 2: Dol-Combourg in pictures

Feudal motte and the moat in the forest of Coëtquen

The ramparts of Dol-de-Bretagne

In the forest of Mesnil, the Fairies' House (covered alley grave)

Mont Dol: the Devil's seat

Combourg: the Templars' courtyard

Saint Lunaire, a Welsh bishop contemporary with Saint Samson, founded a monastery at Combourg in the 6th century, on the spot of a miraculous spring in place Piquette. Four Roman miles away, that is to say 5928 metres, according to the Life of the saint, a stone marked the boundary of his territory. This is to the nearest meter, the distance of the *menhir* de la Butte, at Cuguen. Magical. Like Merlin, the saint has a stag as companion.

Books by Wendy Mewes

Spirit of Place in Finistère (2017, Red Dog Books)
The Nantes-Brest Canal: a guide (3rd edition 2016, Red Dog Books)
Brittany: a cultural history (2014, Signal Books)
The Saints' Shore Way (2013, Red Dog Books)
Legends of Brittany (2012, Red Dog Books)
Brittany (2010, Footprint Guides)
Discovering the History of Brittany (2006, Red Dog Books)

For a full list of publications, please see **www.wendymewes.com**

© 2017, Christophe Déceneux
Éditeur : BoD-Books on Demand,
12/14 rond point des Champs Élysées, 75008 Paris, France
Impression : BoD-Books on Demand, Norderstedt, Allemagne
ISBN : 978-2-322-15651-1
Dépôt légal : avril 2017